an Earth-Friendly Lifestyle

Don Lotter
with
Greg Peterson

Urban Farm Press
Phoenix, AZ

How Green Am I?
Simple Steps to Cultivating
an Earth-Friendly Lifestyle
is adapted from EarthScore:
Your Personal Environmental Audit & Guide
Copyright © 1993 by Donald Lotter.
All Rights Reserved.

Cover design - Parri Willie & Bethany Fisher
Cover layout - Bethany Fisher
Editing - Kathy Davidson, Kaylie Nykai, Courtney Dykstra

Fourth Printing: April 2012
ISBN 978-0-9841788-2-7

To purchase books wholesale contact:
Urban Farm Press
5555 N 7th Street • Suite 134-144
Phoenix, AZ 85014 • 602-279-3713
http://www.UrbanFarmPress.com

Sign up today for our
educational email series
15 Essentials to
Living a Green Lifestyle

Living a green lifestyle comes with a lot of choices, many of them confusing. How do you trust what a company claims about a product? Author Greg Peterson has created a series of emails designed to inspire you into your own level of greenness. His number one rule is "no suffering allowed!" For more information visit:
www.YourGuideToGreen.com/15

****

The Urban Farm's
Simple Sustainability Book Series
is available for
purchase online at
http://www.UrbanFarmPress.com

Table of Contents

Quick Start Guide

Step 1
Locate the worksheet that
lives on page 148 of this book.
Make a photocopy of it and use this
format to track your results.

Step 2
Remember this is a learning process.
Don't be hard on yourself.
Start by making simple changes in the
areas that are exciting to you.

Step 3
There is no suffering allowed. Make
choices that empower you and have fun.

Step 4
Repeat *How Green Am I?* again every
three to six months to see how you
are greening your life.

Forward

People often approach me and say something like, "I can't go green because I can't afford solar panels or a new hybrid car." Their only perception of living a green lifestyle is one of spending a large sum of money to purchase the accoutrements of a green lifestyle. When in reality, there are limitless, inexpensive and free opportunities available to us that cultivate a simple and practical green lifestyle every day. You've probably made a "green" choice today and didn't even realize it. The empty milk carton went into the recycling bin, you paid a bill online, you turned the water off while brushing your teeth or maybe you rode your bike to work.

As we continue to move forward with our lives the idea of living a green lifestyle doesn't have to be overwhelming. Simple choices create the pathway that moves us toward building sustainable communities, and a world capable of meeting the needs of the present without compromising the needs of the future. So how do we nurture the concept of green living in our day-to-day lives? Easy. Ask yourself the question, "How green am I?"

A few years ago the notion of our environmental footprint was created. Our "footprint" is the personal impact we make each day. Our challenge is answering just how we go about measuring our individual footprint?

To assist you in this journey we have brought you *How Green Am I?* Its intent is to help you distinguish the different choices you can make to positively impact and reduce your personal footprint. Use this book as one of your feedback mechanisms to make daily improvements. Might I even suggest that you create a small group of friends to work through the *How Green Am I?* workbook. Read it together and discuss the different things that you can do to lighten your load.

When practicing the concept of reducing your environmental footprint it is most effective to view it as a process, rather than a place to go. A key component of this process is the understanding that your life is a series of choices that are either more or less green (having a bigger or smaller impact). At the same time, it's important to realize that every effort made, no matter how small, makes a difference.

Start with small changes and build from there. For example, begin by replacing your light bulbs with CFL or LED light bulbs. This creates change in the world by saving energy, in many cases reducing the need to burn coal, and saves you money on your electricity bill. As an added bonus, many states and power companies have made these bulbs more affordable by offering price reductions right at the cash register.

Another one of my favorite simple solutions is to NEVER use another plastic water bottle again. There are many facets of this choice that affect your health, pocketbook and the environment. See question 10.7 for more information regarding plastic bottles or visit :

YourGuideToGreen.com/stainless

I also have developed feedback mechanisms in my life. These are subtle reminders of my progress that motivate me to continue the process of improving my effectiveness in living green. One of my favorites is the gas-usage monitoring system in my car. A gauge is located on the dashboard that provides real-time information about my gasoline consumption. This gives me the power to make choices as I drive — accelerate quickly and use a lot of gas, or drive more slowly and use less gas. This has had an unintended effect on my life. Recently, I was driving someone else's car and realized that I was driving it like I drive my own; conserving gas at every turn. That feedback mechanism reached beyond my vehicle and made a difference elsewhere. Where can you put a feedback mechanism in place to help you improve?

Remember my Cardinal Rule, "Living a green lifestyle is not about suffering or doing without." If we are to create a green-living model that works for us it cannot be based on suffering in any way. So remember to have fun with this. Make it a challenge to stretch your ability to live green.

When you begin to realize all of the simple things that you can do to make a positive impact, you likely won't want to stop. Remember, don't overwhelm yourself. Pick one green thing to do and get really good at it, then add more as you progress.

Greg Peterson
The Urban Farmer

Introduction
Your Connections to the Earth

For the majority of people who have been relatively honest with themselves, taking this audit should not be an experience of feeling guilty. Awareness, even without the ability or willingness to change, is important because the process of becoming aware allows the seed for change to be planted. The change could come five years down the road, or it could happen very quickly. So even if you have a high-impact lifestyle, complete *How Green Am I?* just for fun, and don't feel bad if you can't do much about your impact score at this time. Simply maintaining an awareness of your various impact levels in the back of your mind, may give you the opportunity to make changes in the future.

How Green Am I? addresses two areas and consists of 107 questions in 14 sections. There are two types of questions: Impact and Action.

❏ Impact questions measure your environmental impact — how much you impact the earth.

→ Action questions measure the good things you do to affect the environment.

At the end of each section, total your Impact and Action points separately. At the end of the book, add all of the section totals to get a grand total for each category. That score determines your Impact Rating, which ranges from Eco-Titan to Eco-Tyrannosaurus Rex.

Impact points approximate your impact on the environment based on three criteria: (1) pollution, (2) use of non-renewable resources, and (3) degradation of ecological systems. As mentioned previously, these impacts occur both directly and indirectly from the various choices you make.

Action points account for the positive actions you take on behalf of the environment, such as environmental advocacy, education, or setting an example (being a role model). These positive actions may have an environmental impact, such as traveling to a cleanup project, but the benefit of your action hopefully outweighs any negative environmental impacts.

How Green Am I? is meant to be completed multiple times, as frequently as every few months, so that you can track your changes and improvements.

Go to www.UrbanFarmPress.com for a copy of a chart to complete. You can reuse the chart by writing with a different color pencil each subsequent time.

After summing up the section totals, you fill out the chart, which gives you a graphic display of your various impacts and actions. This helps you to visualize your connections and set goals for yourself or your family. To facilitate the development of your personal environmental awareness, you can post your *How Green Am I?* chart in a visible place.

Impact and Action Points are based on the formulas used in the EnviroAccount software. These were developed using environmental information from current books and journals and were further refined based on feedback from the users of EnviroAccount. Impact and Action Points are not meant to be accurate and precise, as accuracy and precision do not yet exist in the newly developing field of impact assessment. For this reason, categories throughout *How Green Am I?* often are not mutually exclusive (that is, $15-$30, followed by $30-$60 rather than $15.99 or $29.99 and so on). Such conciseness would falsely impart an impression of precision. All quantities in *How Green Am I?*, including scores, should be considered approximations. The more important issue is to get a rough, quantitative handle on your relative environmental impact so that you can monitor your progress.

A good example of the comparison of lifestyles is seen between country dwellers and city dwellers. City dwellers (not suburban dwellers) often think of themselves as being environmentally "bad" because they live in the "polluted" city, while country dwellers generally feel the opposite because they live in a more pristine environment. However, upon analysis using EnviroAccount or *How Green Am I?*, the city dwellers often have a significantly lower environmental impact due to their compact habitations and the long distances country dwellers generally drive to commute into the cities.

Most questions are followed by information about why the question is important and what you can do to improve. Additionally, extensive online resources are available at UrbanFarmPress.com with web links so that you can further explore most topics.

Use this time to hone your skills at growing into a greener lifestyle. Remember that it is a process and most of all have fun.

Don Lotter
Davis, California

Section 1
Household Energy:
General

The first three sections of *How Green Am I?* address household energy use, including heating and cooling. Our homes consume the third largest amount of energy just behind the industrial and transportation sectors of the United States economy. By far the greatest share of household energy goes toward heating and cooling. In the 1990's the top eight consumers of home energy were:

1. Heating
2. Water heaters
3. Refrigerator/freezers
4. Air conditioners
5. Ranges
6. Lights
7. Televisions
8. Washers & Dryers

1.1 ❑ IMPACT - Your Energy Bill

My average monthly energy bill, per person, is approximately_____.

1. less than $15	6
2. $15 - $30	12
3. $30 - $60	18
4. $60 - $90	24
5. $90 - $120	30
6. $120 - $150	40
7. $150 - $180	50
8. more than $180	60

My Score_____

☛ Home energy use can be reduced by an estimated 40% to 70% through proper maintenance and upgrades to energy-efficient appliances.

1.2 ❑ IMPACT - Light Bulbs

I have installed energy-saving CFL or LED lights in_____ of my commonly used light fixtures.

1. 3/4	1
2. 1/2	2
3. 1/4	3
4. none	4

My Score_____

☞ Conventional incandescent light bulbs use five to ten times the electricity used by the newer CFL or LED light bulbs. In addition, both CFLs and LEDs last longer making them well worth the investment. If you need a conventional bulb, halogens are the most energy efficient. Incandescent light bulbs are best used in areas where you only turn the light on for brief periods of time.

1.3 ❏ IMPACT - Heating Water
My water heater is_____.

1. solar	1
2. gas & insulated	3
3. gas & not insulated	6
4. electric & insulated	9
5. electric & not insulated	12

My Score_____

☛ Water heating generally consumes the home's third largest amount of energy and accounts for about 16% of your total energy use. Heating water with gas is significantly (30%) cheaper than with electricity. If your water heater is not insulated you should purchase a water heater blanket. You also can insulate the pipes leading from the tank. Your water heater thermostat should be turned to 120° F for optimum efficiency. Solar hot-water systems employ technology that transforms and stores the heat from the sun for energy use.

1.4 ❏ IMPACT - Your Refrigerator

I have an energy-saver refrigerator. I keep it at optimum temperature (30° to 40° F), and I unplug the extra refrigerator if it is not fully used.

1. all of the above/true	1
2. two of the above/true	2
3. one of the above/true	3
4. none of the above/true	4

My Score_____

☛ If you live in a city your refrigerator probably consumes about 15% of your electricity. The most efficient models are in the 16-20 cubic ft range. Side-by-side models are 7% to 13% less energy efficient than bottom freezer models. Any refrigerator with an ice-maker uses even more energy. Maintaining a temperature of 37-40° F for the fresh-food compartment and 0-5° F for the freezer will save energy.

1.5 → ACTION - Renewable Energy

I have invested _____ effort/money in installing solar energy equipment around my home in order to reduce my dependence on energy from non-renewable sources.

1. no	0
2. a little	3
3. moderate	6
4. fairly extensive	9
5. a great deal of	12

My Score_____

☛ Passive solar heating can cut your heating costs up to 50% over heating that does not incorporate passive solar design techniques.

1.6 → ACTION - Appliances
I have invested_____ in energy-saving appliances for my home.

1. none/very little	0
2. a little	3
3. moderately	6
4. fairly extensively	9
5. a great deal	12

My Score_____

☞ Generally, the most important appliance for energy savings is the refrigerator, but there are many additional ways to save energy in the kitchen. For instance, use a microwave instead of your oven, purchase a solar oven, or install an outdoor kitchen, to name a few.

1.7 → ACTION

During sunny weather, I _____ dry my clothes on a clothesline.

1. never	0
2. occasionally	1
3. frequently	2
4. usually	3
5. always	4

My Score_____

☛ On a warm sunny day, producing heat to dry clothes is a waste of energy. This is particularly true if you're using air conditioning since the clothes dryer may be heating up the air you are paying to cool.

Total Your Scores For Section 1

❏ IMPACT _____

→ ACTION _____

Section 2
Household Energy:
Winter

If you want to reduce your home-energy use, winter heating and heat conservation are the first places to look. In colder climates, up to 60% of total household energy can go to heating the home. This section evaluates your efforts to conserve heat energy.

At the end of this section you will rate the winter coldness for your area from very cold to warm and then reduce or increase your points accordingly.

2.1 ❏ IMPACT

In winter, during waking hours, I keep the house temperature around ___ degrees F.

1. 64 or below	2
2. 64-66	4
3. 66-68	6
4. 68-70	8
5. 70 or above	10

My Score_____

☛ Pile-lined clothing is great for keeping warm around the house and saving energy. Fleece is light and comfortable and can pay for itself in one winter's energy savings. Remember wearing more clothes is an excellent way to save dollars on your heating bill.

2.2 ❑ IMPACT

In winter, during sleeping hours, I keep the house temperature around __ degrees F.

1. 55 or below	2
2. 55-59	4
3. 59-62	6
4. 62-66	8
5. 66 or above	10

My Score_____

☛ Do not sleep under an electric blanket. Research indicates that the electromagnetic field (EMF) generated can be a health hazard and can disrupt the immune systems of those sleeping under them when they are turned on. Children and pregnant women in particular should avoid electric blankets. It is considered safe to warm a bed with an electric blanket before you get into it, as long as it is turned off when you get in.

2.3 ❑ IMPACT

The size of my living space is approximately_____. (Divide your total living space by the number of people living in it.)

1. 300 sq. ft. or less (17 feet by 17 feet)	3
2. 300 - 600 sq. ft.	6
3. 600 - 900 sq. ft.	9
4. 900 - 1500 sq. ft.	12
5. more than 1500 sq ft.	15

My Score_____

☛ For many people, co-housing and shared living spaces are important ways to reduce environmental impacts with the added benefit of improving social interaction. Shared living means using less energy, space and "things" (such as vacuum cleaners, freezers, and toys) per person. Shared housing, cooperative communities, co-housing, and village clusters are approaches currently being practiced and developed.

2.4 ❑ IMPACT

The house I live in is insulated_____.

1. very well, including walls, ceiling, dual-pane windows	2
2. well	4
3. fairly well	8
4. poorly	10

My Score_____

Those who use little or no heating in winter should answer 1 or 2.

☛ If you plan to insulate, take the time to learn about different materials. For example, foam insulation often is made from chlorofluorocarbons (CFCs) or other ozone-depleting chemicals. Other types of insulation, such as spun glass or cellulose, may be more appropriate.

If you have an attic, be sure that it is insulated. The minimum recommended R value for insulation is R-30.

Ten times as much heat escapes from a single-pane window as through a wall. Drapes can reduce the heat lost through a window by 50% if the drapes are insulated. Double-pane windows and reflective coatings also are effective at cutting heat loss.

****

2.5 ❑ IMPACT

The doors, windows, pipes and electrical outlets in my house are caulked, weather-stripped, or sealed_____.

1. very well	1
2. well	2
3. adequately	3
4. poorly	4

My Score_____

☛ Energy and construction experts explain that the cracks and gaps in many U.S. homes are equivalent to having a 3-foot-by-3-foot hole in the wall. This translates to a loss of approximately 15% of home heating energy. These holes can be sealed with caulk. Doors and window frames can be sealed with specially designed weather-stripping, available at hardware stores. Depending on the time of year, you can check for leaks by standing close to doors and windows and feeling for hot or cold air coming in around the tops and sides of each opening. Applying caulking and weather-stripping to leaky doors and windows can result in up to a 10% savings in energy costs. According to experts, 99% of all houses in the U.S. with central furnaces or air conditioners have duct leaks.

Balance weather-stripping and sealing your house with adequate ventilation to prevent the build-up of gases emanating from foam insulation, carpets, particle board, and so on. In some cases, indoor air can be the source of 90% of the air pollution we breathe. A heat-exchange system may be recommended.

2.6 ❑ IMPACT

I burn _____ cords of firewood per year. (A full-size pickup truck holds about a half cord. A full cord is equal to 4 ft x 4 ft x 8 ft area.)

1. 0	0
2. less than 1/2	2
3. 1/2 -1	4
4. 1 - 2	6
5. 2 - 3	8
6. more than 3	10

My Score_____

☛ If you have an Environmental Protection Agency (EPA)-certified catalytic stove, divide points by 3. The burning of wood can be a serious source of local air pollution. The points given here are for this pollution, not for energy use. A catalytic stove actually re-burns the smoke particles and emits a fraction of the pollution of a regular wood burning stove.

2.7 → ACTION

I have had the following type of energy audit done on my house_____.

1. no audit	0
2. informal self-audit	3
3. self-audit with published guide	6
4. free utility company audit	9
5. professional audit	12

My Score_____

☛ Utility companies typically have a home energy self-audit or will make referrals to professional home energy auditors.

2.8 → ACTION

I have invested_____time and/or money to increase energy efficiency and decrease my use of non-renewable energy for heating my home. (Question 1.3 in the previous section determined how much you invest in energy efficient appliances. This question regards energy-efficient heating systems.)

1. no/very little	0
2. some	3
3. moderate	6
4. fairly extensive	9
5. extensive	12

My Score_____

☛ The average retrofit project pays for itself in four years of utility bill savings. Ceiling fans circulate warm air from the ceiling, which can be 15° F warmer than the air at floor level. A ceiling fan takes about the same amount of energy as an incandescent light bulb. When purchasing ceiling fans, look for the Energy Star label. Not only do these ceiling fans move at least 20% more air per watt of power consumed, but they use 60% to 70% less electricity for lighting than equivalent incandescent models.

Ceiling fan designs with built-in ballasts and pin-based fluorescent lamps will be more energy-efficient than ones with screw-based compact fluorescent bulbs.

Passive solar heat gain occurs when the sun warms your house, and that heat is stored for use after dark.

Furnaces need to be "tuned up" occasionally. This can be done by a heating technician for $35-$100 depending on your system and where you live. Changing your air filter regularly will help increase furnace and air conditioner efficiency. Invest in a washable filter and clean it often for further savings of money and earth resources.

Total Your Scores For Section 2

❏ IMPACT_____

➔ ACTION_____

Now choose a winter-coldness rating for your area from the following categories (these are multipliers, not points).

2.0 - Very cold winters (average minimum temperatures below 10° F)

1.5 - Cold winters (average minimum temperatures between 10° F and 20° F)

1.0 - Average winters (average minimum temperatures between 20° F and 30° F)

0.75 - Cool winters (average minimum temperatures between 30° F and 40° F)

0.50 - Warm winters (average minimum temperatures above 40° F)

Enter your winter-coldness rating____

Now multiply to get ADJUSTED IMPACT POINTS_____

Section 3
Household Energy:
Summer

Electricity (typically made from burning coal) to run your air conditioner is a major home energy draw during summer. It is especially environmentally costly because demand comes during the afternoon at a time when electric power plants are overloaded. During these "peak hours" utility companies must start up their oil burning plants to provide the extra electricity. This section evaluates your use of air conditioning and your efforts to minimize the use of energy for cooling your house.

3.1 ❑ IMPACT

On summer days, I use air-condition-ing____.

1. never	0
2. 10-20 days/yr.	5
3. 21-30 days/yr.	10
4. 31-50 days/yr.	15
5. just about every day	20

My Score_____

☞ There are many ways to cool a house naturally to delay or prevent the need for turning on the air conditioner. A fan, including ceiling fans, uses about one-tenth of the energy of an air conditioner. Open the windows at night to cool your home then close them in the morning to retain cool air.

Strategically planted deciduous trees (to allow sunlight in winter and provide shade in the summer) can go a long way toward keeping a house cool and comfortable. In non-humid regions, such as the Western United States, swamp coolers that blow water-cooled air are effective, energy efficient, and underutilized.

Do you set the thermostat as high as possible (78° F)? Is your air conditioner shaded? (It should be.) Do you turn off the air conditioner when you leave the house for more than a half hour? Do you keep your air conditioner's coils clean and straight? Do you choose re-usable filters and keep them clean? All these strategies will assist in reducing electricity consumption.

****

3.2 ❏ IMPACT
On summer nights, I use air conditioning_____.

1. never	0
2. 10 - 20 nights/yr	5
3. 20 - 40 nights/yr	10
4. 40 - 60 nights/yr	15
5. just about every night	20

My Score_____

3.3 ❏ IMPACT

In the summer, I reduce my use of electricity during the peak hours of noon to 6 P.M.____.

1. always	1
2. most of the time	2
3. frequently	3
4. sometimes	4
5. rarely or never	5

My Score_____

☛ When you use electricity during peak hours, along with many other people, utility companies often have to start up power plants that must burn oil, which is both economically and environmentally costly. Peak-hour rates can cost 4 times more per kilowatt hour than the lowest night rates.

3.4 → ACTION

The east, south and west facing windows of my house are _____ shaded by trees, awnings, and trellises to keep direct sunlight out of the house during summer.

1. not at all	0
2. slightly	1
3. half	2
4. mostly	3
5. thoroughly	4

My Score_____

☛ For a passive solar application, plant trees that shade your home in the summer and shed their leaves in winter to allow the passage of sunlight into the house. This helps keep your home warm in the winter and cool in the summer.

3.5 → ACTION

During the summer, I make____ effort to increase my tolerance to heat by strategies such as performing regular moderate exercise, reducing sugar and fat in my diet, eating plenty of fresh fruit, and drinking lots of water.

1. no	0
2. a little	4
3. a moderate	6
4. a good	8
5. a great	10

My Score_____

☛ You will be surprised how well diet and exercise work to increase your tolerance for heat. Start exercising easily and build up.

3.6 → ACTION

In the summer, I use a solar cooker to cook my food___.

1. never	0
2. once a month or less	1
3. once a week	2
4. twice a week	3
5. more than twice a week	4

My Score_____

☞ Solar cooking saves energy in two places: at the oven and at the air conditioner. Cooking with the sun helps to keep the temperature of your home down by eliminating the need to use the oven. Many people use solar ovens at least once a week, and the food they cook using this method often tastes better than anything cooked in a conventional oven.

Total Your Scores for Section 3

❏ IMPACT_____

→ ACTION_____

Section 4
Water

Water is absolutely central to life. We are made of it, we cleanse ourselves with it, we play in it, and we use it in a thousand different ways. Yet despite its centrality to our existence, water is one of the most poorly managed of our resources.

Developing good water-use habits is of utmost importance, especially in the Western United States, where the availability and use of water looms as the major political and environmental issue of the future.

This section evaluates your water use and your efforts to conserve. At the end of this section you will be asked to rate water scarcity for your region. You will then increase or reduce your water points accordingly. If you are in a region with plenty of water, Impact Points for water use will be minimal.

4.1 ❑ IMPACT

My watered lawn and garden space is
____. (Exclude food gardens.)

1. less than 200 sq. ft.	2
2. 200-500 sq. ft.	4
3. 500-1,000 sq. ft.	8
4. 1,000-3,000 sq. ft.	16
5. more than 3,000 sq. ft.	32

My Score_____

☛ Lawns and gardens commonly account for 80% of water used in a household. A week of watering your lawn can use 1000's of gallons. Inefficient watering or hot spells can double these numbers. Decreasing the frequency of your lawn mowing also will help reduce water needs. Raising the blade of your mower, to at least three inches, will maintain longer leaf surfaces and thus require less water to keep it green and healthy. Watering in the early morning or at night reduces the amount of water that evaporates before water gets into the soil.

4.2 ❑ IMPACT

I_____.

1. do not have a swimming
   pool   0
2. have a swimming pool
   that doesn't leak   4
3. have a swimming pool
   that leaks a little   6
4. have a swimming pool
   that leaks a lot   8

My Score_____

☛ Approximately one in 20 pools leaks. Just a small leak in a pool can result in the loss of 700 gallons of water a day. If your pool loses more than a quarter inch of water per day (a half inch in hot, dry regions), you probably have a leak. Covering the pool may help reduce water loss through evaporation by up to 90%.

4.3 ❏ IMPACT

I use _____ water to wash my car and other outside things like my patio.

1. no	0
2. a little	1
3. a moderate amount of	2
4. a lot of	3

My Score_____

☛ Check for leaks in your hoses and use shut-off/trigger nozzles that completely turn off the water when not in use to minimize the wasting of water.

4.4 ❑ IMPACT

Leaky faucets or pipes in my house or on my property cause__ water waste.

1. no or very little	0
2. a little	2
3. some	4
4. a fair amount of	6
5. extensive	8

My Score_____

☛ A small leak from a faucet can waste 50 gallons of water per day. A leaky toilet can waste 8,000 gallons a month. To identify a toilet leak, put some food coloring in the tank. If it shows up in the bowl without flushing, you have a leak. To reduce the amount of water used per flush put a plastic bottle full of water, a brick or dam in the toilet tank. Non-low-flow toilets use 5-7 gallons per flush and these methods help to reduce that. Installing a low flow toilet can reduce the amount of water use by up to 3.4 gallons per flush.

4.5 → ACTION

I have installed low-flow showerheads and low-volume flush devices on my toilets.

1. None of the above are true	0
2. One of the above is true	1
3. Two of the above are true	2
4. This is true of all of my showers and toilets	3

My Score_____

☞ Faucet aerators reduce flow by 50% yet maintain good pressure and cost just a few dollars apiece. Look for aerators that deliver 0.5 to 1 gallon per minute. A low-flow showerhead that costs between $7-$20, pays for itself in just a few months and uses no more that 2.5 gallons per minute at standard residential water pressure. This represents about 50% reduction of water use.

4.6 → ACTION

Such strategies as planting drought- resistant lawn and garden plants (xeriscaping), using drip irrigation, planting trees and using other techniques, have helped reduced my water consumption_____.

1. not at all	0
2. a little	3
3. moderately	6
4. very significantly	9
5. greatly	12

My Score_____

☛ Xeriscaping is an innovative strategy that significantly reduces water usage. The xeriscape approach takes into account planning and design, soil and turf area analysis, suitable plant selections, efficient irrigation practices and systems, and the use of mulches when designing lawns and gardens.

4.7 → ACTION

I have invested _____in water-saving technologies such as greywater systems and ultralow-flow toilets.

1. nothing or very little	0
2. a little	2
3. moderately	4
4. extensively	6
5. very extensively	8

My Score_____

☛ A greywater system saves shower, sink and clothes wash water from your house to use for watering your landscape. Do not however use blackwater -- the water from toilets and the kitchen sink.

4.8 → ACTION

I make _____ effort to conserve water by doing such things as minimizing my shower flow and flushing every other time I use the toilet.

1. no or very little	0
2. some	1
3. a moderately good	2
4. a really good	3
5. a great	4

My Score_____

Total Your Scores for Section 4

❏ IMPACT_____

→ ACTION_____

On a scale of 0.25 to 3.0 rate the water scarcity for your area and enter it below.

   0.25 (water very plentiful all year)
   0.5 (water fairly plentiful)
   1.0 (some scarcity of water)
   2.0 (water scarce)
   3.0 (water very scarce)

Examples: Southern California & Arizona = 3; San Francisco Bay Area = 2.0; Atlantic seaboard = 0.5 to 1.0

Enter your water scarcity rating:

_____

Enter your Impact Point total for this section: _____

Now multiply these to get adjusted Impact points: _____

Section 5
Transportation

Operating an automobile has a greater environmental impact than any other common human activity except for having children. According to Department of Energy 2008 figures, transportation accounts for 71% of US oil consumption and is the predominant source of air pollution. In urban areas, one third to one half of all land is given over to the automobile in some way: for streets, parking lots, gas stations, repair shops, junkyards, and so on. This section evaluates your transportation energy use and efforts to promote efficiency and minimize pollution.

5.1 ❏ IMPACT

My main vehicle gets _____ miles per gallon of gasoline.

1. I don't own a car	0
2. I have an electric car	1
3. 45 or more	3
4. 35-45	6
5. 25-35	9
6. 15-25	12
7. less than 15	15

My Score_____

☛ Keeping your car well tuned is the best way to get good mileage. Other strategies are to keep tires properly inflated, keep your speed down, and refrain from warming up the engine when you start. Maintaining a driving speed of 55 mph on the highways will optimize fuel efficiency. There is a 20% loss of fuel economy when driving at 75 mph versus 55 mph. Avoid rapid acceleration and stops.

5.2 ❑ IMPACT

I drive _____ miles per year. (If you share a car with another person, then divide the total mileage by 2.)

1. 0-1,000	4
2. 1,000-4,000	8
3. 4,000-8,000	16
4. 8,000-12,000	24
5. 12,000-16,000	32
6. 16,000-20,000	40
7. 20,000-24,000	48
8. 24,000-30,000	56
9. more than 30,000	64

My Score_____

☛ Driving can be put on a highly subjective continuum between two poles: necessary and unnecessary. Unnecessary driving is a tough habit to break, and a very personal decision. Begin to weigh what your personal boundaries are and implement that which works for you.

5.3 ❑ IMPACT

The engine in my vehicle is in _____ condition.

1. new or newly rebuilt	2
2. good	4
3. fair	6
4. poor	8
5. bad	10

My Score_____

☛ Your car's emissions will be much higher if its engine is old and in poor condition.

5.4 ❏ IMPACT

I have my car tuned_____.

1. as recommended in the owner's manual	0
2. when it's hard to start	10
3. when it breaks down	20

My Score_____

☛ By far the most important issue for keeping emissions down (and getting good mileage) is whether the car's engine is in good condition and kept well tuned. According to the Environmental Protection Agency, if you have an older car, keeping it well tuned can reduce pollution by 40%.

5.5 ❏ IMPACT

I take an average of ___short distance car trips (less than 2 miles) per week.

1. less than 3	2
2. 4-8	5
3. 9-12	10
4. 13-18	15
5. more than 18 a week	20

My Score_____

☛ When your engine runs cold, which it does on a trip of less than 2 miles, pollutant emissions are much higher. These short-distance trips produce up to 40% of vehicle pollution in urban areas. Try to incorporate your driving errands and grocery shopping into your commute home from work.

5.6 ❑ IMPACT

The fuel I use in my car is_____.

1. electric car	1
2. bio-fuel (methanol, ethanol, natural gas) or hybrid electric	2
3. a mixture of bio-fuel and unleaded gasoline	3
4. unleaded gasoline- low octane	4
5. unleaded gasoline- high octane	6
6. leaded gasoline	10

My Score_____

☛ High-octane gasoline contains compounds that are among the worst environmental pollutants: benzene, xylene, and toluene. Experts state that octane is only beneficial for certain high compression engines and is greatly overused. Do not use mid-grade or premium grade unless specified in the owner's manual.

Higher octane gasoline alone does not run "cleaner".

Hybrids combine small, internal combustion engines with electric motors and electricity storage devices. They contain intelligent power electronics that "decide" when to use the motor and engine and when it is more appropriate to use the electricity or store it in the batteries for future use. Hybrids also reduce emissions.

****

5.7 ❑ IMPACT
I drive alone____ % of my total driving miles.

1. 0-20	2
2. 20-40	4
3. 40-60	6
4. 60-80	8
5. 80-100	10

My Score_____

5.8 ❏ IMPACT

I have_____ other motor-driven vehicles (boat, snowmobile, motorcycle, seated lawn mower, airplane, recreational vehicle, and so on).

1. 0	0
2. 1	4
3. 2	8
4. 3	12
5. 4 or more	16

My Score_____

5.9 ❏ IMPACT

For this question add up the approximate number of miles you have flown in the last 5 years and then divide by 5 to find your 5-year average. I travel_____ miles per year by air.

1. 0-1,000	1
2. 1,000-5,000	2
3. 5,000-10,000	4
4. 10,000-20,000	8
5. 20,000-30,000	16
6. 30,000-50,000	32
7. more than 50,000	48

My Score_____

☛ If you travel as a passenger on an airliner at near-full passenger capacity, you use about the same amount of fuel as if you drive a car (by yourself) that gets 27 miles per gallon. It is much easier to log several thousand miles per week of flying, than of driving, however.

5.10 → ACTION
I carpool for _____ % of my commuting miles annually.

1. 0	0
2. 1-20	5
3. 20-40	10
4. 40-60	15
5. 60-80	25
6. 80-100	30

My Score_____

5.11 → ACTION

I use mass transit for _____ % of my commuting miles.

1. 0	0
2. 1-20	5
3. 20-40	10
4. 40-60	15
5. 60-80	25
6. 80-100	30

My Score_____

☛ Van pooling and mass transit provide great opportunities for catching up on reading and work that you couldn't do while driving.

The following is an early 1990's list that illustrates the average amount of pollution emitted from urban U.S. transport modes for a typical work commute. Grams of carbon per passenger mile: rapid rail 0.3; light rail 0.4; transit bus 20.0; vanpool 36.0; carpool 70.0; automobile 209.0.

5.12 → ACTION
I do _____% of my commuting miles by bicycle or on foot.

1. 0	0
2. 1-20	5
3. 20-40	10
4. 40-60	15
5. 60-80	25
6. 80-100	30

My Score_____

☛ The distance between where you live and work is an important factor in your environmental impact. City dwellers can score very well in this question because many of them have a short commute while others find that they can live well without owning a car at all.

On the other hand, country dwellers often work in cities and commute long distances despite the fact that they originally moved to the countryside partly to become environmentally "sensible".

5.13 → ACTION
I travel____% of my around-town miles by bicycle or by foot.

1. 0	0
2. 1-20	5
3. 20-40	10
4. 40-60	15
5. 60-80	25
6. 80-100	30

My Score_____

☛Does your city have a bicycle program? Citizen pressure is important in developing programs for bicycle paths and alternative transportation incentives.

5.14 → ACTION
When I travel by air I make _____ effort to fly by the most fuel-efficient aircraft available.

1. no	0
2. a little	5
3. a moderate	10
4. a good	15
5. an extensive	25

My Score_____

☛New aircraft are the most fuel efficient, up to 40% more so than older ones. Some airlines will be introducing aircraft with engines that have significantly lower emissions of NOx's, a pollutant that is linked to the destruction of the ozone layer. Public inquiry will make a difference in whether airline companies decide to invest in these technologies.

Total Your Scores For Section 5

❏ IMPACT_____

→ ACTION_____

Section 6
Consumerism: Durable Goods

The buying of consumer goods has a major impact on the environment, and is probably the most complex to assess. According to the 2000 Report Card for America's Infrastructure & Solid Waste the U.S. generated approximately 4.5 pounds of waste per person per day, a total of 232 million tons.

The industrial sector, much of which manufactures consumer goods, uses more energy than any other. An imbalance exists because our economic system has not developed to the point where the consumer pays for all the environmental impacts of producing and disposing of an item. These "hidden" environmental costs are called "externalities."

This section evaluates your general level of consumerism and your efforts to reduce the environmental impact of your consumption.

6.1 ❏ IMPACT

I am a _____shopper/buyer of durable goods (not counting secondhand goods). Durable goods include clothing, electronic goods, vehicles, toys, appliances, furniture, recreational items, tools, and so on, but do not count food. (Families divide the total expenditures by the number of adults.)

1. very light
   ($50/mo. avg. or less)   16
2. light
   ($50-$150/mo. avg.)   24
3. moderate
   ($150-$300/mo. avg.)   32
4. moderately heavy
   ($300-$500/mo. avg.)   48
5. heavy
   ($500-$800/mo. avg.)   64
6. very heavy (more than $800/mo.
   avg.)   96

My Score_____

☛This question has to do with your role in the environmental impact of the production (resource extraction, processing, and transport) of goods. An identical question in the waste section gives IMPACT points for the disposal of these items.

****

6.2 ❏ IMPACT
In the past 5 years, I have purchased _____ new or almost new motor vehicles. (Almost new means 2 years old or less. Do not count vehicles that were more than 2 years old when purchased.)

1. 0	0
2. 1	6
3. 2	12
4. 3	18
5. 4	24

My Score_____

☛The manufacture of an automobile consumes enormous amounts of energy and raw materials, including the following (figures from the 1990's):

- steel (1,500-3,500 lb.)
- plastic and composite synthetic materials (200-1,000 lb.)
- glass, aluminum, and other materials (120-200 lb.)

A single car contains four to ten times more plastic than all other types of plastic that you are likely to consume in a year.

In addition, the manufacture of the average 2,370-pound car generates nearly 27 tons of waste: metals, plastics, glass, and so on. Every time a new vehicle is purchased it sends a message back to the manufacturer to produce another vehicle, which in turn sends a message even further back in the process to extract more resources (ore, petroleum, and so on). Depending on how much you drive, it is sometimes better, from an environmental point of view, to keep an older car that is running well and uses unleaded fuel, than to buy a new car that gets just a few more miles per gallon.

6.3 → ACTION

When I want to acquire something, I make_____ effort to purchase a second-hand product by going to thrift stores and checking classified ads.

1. no	0
2. a little	4
3. a moderate	8
4. a good	16
5. an extensive	32

My Score_____

☛Enough people exerting enough economic demand for second-hand goods places value on well-made products, which in turn gives companies incentives to produce them.

Many cities have salvage centers and businesses that specialize in all kinds of second-hand items, especially for home construction.

6.4 → ACTION

When I want to acquire something, I make _____ effort to buy goods made from low-impact, recycled, or renewable materials or, from companies that have a good environmental record.

1. no	0
2. a little	3
3. a moderate	6
4. a good	12
5. extensive	24

My Score_____

6.5 ACTION

I make _____ effort to inform store managers and owners that I am interested in buying products made from low-impact, recycled, or renewable materials and from companies that have a good environmental record.

1. no	0
2. a little	2
3. a moderate	4
4. a good	8
5. an extensive	16

My Score_____

☛Information is increasingly available on the ways we can choose to consume and help bring about a lower environmental impact. Corporations are extremely sensitive to consumer choice and awareness. Do not underestimate the power of your dollar, the impact of talking to the manager of your favorite restaurant or your telephone call.

Total Your Scores For Section 6

❏ IMPACT_____

→ ACTION_____

Section 7
Consumerism:
Food and Agricultural Products

Food is our most fundamental connection to the earth. We transform the land with our agriculture and with its harvest we take in the earth's nutrients and energy to feed ourselves. Consequently, selecting the food you eat deserves special care. Food that is grown using organic fertilizers and ecologically based methods of pest control is worth its moderately higher price.

This section evaluates your impact when buying at the grocery store, and it assesses your efforts to support ecological sustainability in food and agricultural products. Consumption of organically grown food minimizes your Impact Points in this section whereas high levels of consumption of meat and extensively processed foods can combine to give you high Impact Points.

7.1 ❏ IMPACT

I _____ eat canned, frozen, and individually packaged foods.

1. never/rarely	1
2. sometimes (1 meal/wk.)	4
3. fairly frequently (2-4 meals/wk.)	8
4. frequently (5-7 meals/wk.)	12
5. usually	16

My Score_____

☛Canning, freezing, processing, and transporting foods use a lot of energy. Food packaging accounts for 30% of U.S. trash by volume.

7.2 ❑ IMPACT

As a percentage of my food dollar, I buy
_____ % organically grown or unsprayed
food.

1. more than 40%	4
2. 30%-40%	8
3. 15%-30%	16
4. 5%-15%	24
5. 0%-5%	32

My Score_____

☛Growing food has a high environmental
impact because of the large amounts of
pesticides and chemical fertilizers that are
applied to the land (1.5 billion pounds per
year). Up to 40% of the pesticide is applied just to make the product look better.
By using existing organic farming techniques we could grow much of our food,
perhaps most of it, without pesticides or
synthetic fertilizers. Organic farming em-
phasizes ecological sustainability, biolog-

ical diversity, and the health of soil, plants, animals, and, therefore, humans.

Ask your local grocer about organically grown produce, and check at health-food stores and farmers' markets.

You can minimize your environmental impact by eating foods that are (1) low on the food chain (vegetarian), (2) minimally processed, (3) organically grown, and/or (4) locally produced.

****

7.3 ❏ IMPACT

I eat _____ pound(s) of beef per week.

1. 0	0
2. less than 1/4	4
3. 1/4-1/2	8
4. 1/2-1	16
5. 1-2	24
6. 2-3	32
7. 3-4	48
8. more than 4	64

My Score_____

☞ The average person in the United States eats 3 to 4 pounds of beef per week. To produce one steak takes an incredible 2,000 gallons of water.

Beef production has the highest environmental impact of any common food, particularly in the western U.S., where water is scarce and livestock graze on fragile semiarid and subalpine lands. According to Jeremy Rifkin, who started the Beyond Beef Campaign, "There is no other force on earth more destructive than the cow, except for the automobile." The goal of the campaign is to influence consumers around the world to cut beef consumption by 50%.

According to the EPA one farm with 2500 cows will produce as much waste as a city of approximately 411,000 people. In 2008, beef and pork consumption is expected to top 280 million tons. One step that can help allay world hunger and the depletion of the earth's resources is reducing human meat consumption by 10%. To produce one pound of meat requires 2,500 to 6,000 pounds of wheat that could be used to feed people starving in other parts of the world.

For those who desire beef, choose companies that specialize in beef production using sustainable grassland grazing (as opposed to grain feeding) and **no** hormones and antibiotics.

****

7.4 ❑ IMPACT

I eat____ pound(s) of non-beef meat per week (chicken, fish, pork, mutton, and so on).

1. 0	0
2. less than 1/4	2
3. 1/4 to 1/2	4
4. 1/2 to 1	8
5. more than 1	16

My Score_____

☛These foods have a lower environmental impact than beef, but a much higher impact than vegetarian foods. The environmental impact of sea fishing varies. Some types of "fish harvesting" are sustainable, while many others are not, depending on the species and the region.

Many stores, especially food co-ops, sell "free range" and hormone-free chicken; poultry raised outside of cages and without the use of drugs or hormones.

****

7.5 → ACTION

I buy_____ of my food from bulk bins or in large packages, or mostly as unprocessed food.

1. none/very little	0
2. some	2
3. moderate amounts	4
4. a good amount	8
5. most	16

My Score_____

7.6 → ACTION

As a percentage of my food dollar, I spend ____ % at the local farmers market or outlet.

1. 0%-5%	0
2. 5%-15%	2
3. 15%-30%	4
4. 30%-40%	8
5. more than 40%	16

My Score_____

☛Support your local food growers. Local, small-scale farming increases ecological diversity and community self-reliance and reduces the need for transporting and refrigerating large amounts of fresh food grown far away.

7.7 → ACTION

I make _____ effort to buy textile products from organically grown or unsprayed cotton or less environmentally costly sources such as wool, linen, hemp, or recycled material, such as plastic.

1. no/very little	0
2. some	5
3. a moderate	10
4. an extensive	20

My Score_____

☛Unsprayed and sustainably produced, ("green") cotton is now becoming available. More pesticides are applied to cotton than to any other crop. Twenty-four percent (24%) of the insecticides sold on the world market in 1994 were used on cotton crops. The cotton-growing areas of the world, whether the lowlands of Guatemala or the San Joaquin Valley of

California, are severely contaminated with pesticides and in some cases are virtual "deserts" because their ecological systems have been so disrupted. The impact of this pesticide use is unknown for other products, such as prepared foods that use cottonseed oil in their manufacture.

Total Your Scores For Section 7

❏ IMPACT_____

→ ACTION_____

Section 8
Consumerism:
Paper and Forest Products

Forest and watershed management in western North America has become increasingly destructive and environmentally unsustainable. Sustainable forestry practices, which have been researched and developed, need to be implemented on a much wider scale. However, this type of sustainable logging will only be widely adopted as a result of consumer demand for recycled paper and sustainably produced lumber products, as well as citizen pressure on the U.S. Forest Service.

This section evaluates your use of paper and forest products as well as your efforts to favor products that create less impact.

8.1 ❑ IMPACT

In my house, we subscribe to _____ daily newspapers per reader.

1. no	0
2. less than 1/4 (4 or more readers/paper)	3
3. 1/3 to 1/2 (2 to 3 readers/paper)	6
4. 1	9
5. 2	12
6. 3 or more	15

My Score_____

☛Paper has three major environmental impacts: (1) destruction of forests, (2) dioxin production during the chlorine bleaching process, and, (3) disposal (some 40% of landfills are paper waste).

One simple thing to do - share a newspaper with a neighbor?

8.2 ❏ IMPACT
In my house, we have ____ magazine subscriptions per reader.

1.	0	0
2.	1-2	3
3.	3-4	6
4.	4-6	9
5.	6-8	12
6.	more than 8	15

My Score_____

☛ Your local library or bookstore will have many of these magazines.

****

8.3 ❏ IMPACT
I am a ____ consumer of paper, other than newspapers and magazines, such as books, photocopies and so on. Check paper used at work for the recycled fiber content listed on the label.

1. very light   3
2. light (1/8" stack = 1/4 lb/wk)   6
3. moderate
     (1/4" stack = 1/2 lb /wk)   9
4. moderately heavy
     (1/2" stack = 1 lb /wk.)   12
5. heavy
     (1" stack = 2 lbs./wk)   15
6. very heavy over 2 pounds.   20

My Score_____

☛ When you photocopy can you use a machine that prints double-sided? Do you request recycled paper? Do you print drafts and internal documents on paper previously printed on one side? For large numbers of such printed materials as flyers, can you reduce the size to fit four on one page and then get the paper cut into quarters? Most copy shops will make such cuts for a small fee.

8.4 ❏ IMPACT

In the past 5 years, my use of forest-grown lumber products has been, on average,_____.

1. very small
   (100 board ft. or less)   2
2. small
   (100-200 board ft.)   4
3. medium
   (500-1,000 board ft.)   8
4. substantial
   (1,000-5,000 board ft.)   16
5. very substantial
   (more than 5,000 board ft.)   32

My Score_____

☛ A small addition to a house might require 500 to 1,000 board feet of lumber, while a major addition might require 1,000 to 5,000 board feet. A new house generally requires 10,000 board feet.

Wood-certification programs, in which

timber operations are inspected as to the sustainability of their practices and given certification if they pass, are a new and important development in the United States. If you are going to have any construction done, it is important that you discuss with your contractor the options for getting sustainably produced wood.

****

8.5 ❏ IMPACT

When I acquire an undomesticated pet such as a bird or a snake, I make ___ effort to be sure that it was bred in captivity and not taken from the wild.

1. no		4
2. a little		3
3. a moderate		2
4. a good		1
5. I do not have any undomesticated pets		0

My Score_____

☛This question can also apply to house plants, such as cacti and to some specialty foods, such as hearts of palm, turtle eggs, and so on.

****

8.6 → ACTION
I make _____ effort to obtain my reading materials (newspapers, magazines, books, and so on) as a multiple user, that is, at libraries, in cafes, from friends, and so on.

1. no/very little	0
2. some	2
3. a moderate	4
4. a good	6
5. an extensive	8

My Score_____

8.7 → ACTION

I make _____ effort to reduce my junk mail.

1. no	0
2. a little	1
3. a moderate	2
4. a good	3
5. an extensive	4

My Score_____

☞ Your receipt of junk mail is considered in your score even though you do not "buy" this material. Each year approximately 53 million trees are cut down for junk mail and over 3.6 million tons of paper are used to print catalogs. Paper for catalogs alone caused the destruction of 74,000 acres of forest in 1992. Consideration should be given, however, to the fact that shopping by catalog can reduce the amount of driving you do, as well as the amount of impulse buying.

8.8 → ACTION

I make _____ effort to buy my paper products from sources that use recycled paper and to let companies know that I want them to print on recycled and chlorine-free paper.

1. no	0
2. a little	1
3. a moderate	2
4. a good	3
5. an extensive	4

My Score_____

☛ To be truly recycled, paper should contain at least 50% "postconsumer" waste. Much of the paper now sold as "recycled" does not meet this criterion and may in fact have no postconsumer paper in it whatsoever. Postconsumer recycling not only saves trees, but reduces the energy used in paper production and reduces air and water pollution. It also reduces the load on landfills, of which paper has been the largest single component.

The Chlorine bleaching of pulp to make

white paper is a major cause of dioxin pollution because wastewater from the bleaching process is dumped into the oceans. You can make your printer and magazine publishers aware of such information. Consumer pressure goes a long way in promoting sustainable-thinking in every industry.

****

8.9 → ACTION

When I have construction done, I make _____ effort to look for a contractor that specializes in environmentally sound building and/or to have the contractor use materials that are low impact (such as earthen materials), sustainably produced, indigenous (locally derived), or salvaged.

1. no	0
2. a little	2
3. a moderate	4
4. a good	6
5. an extensive	8

My Score_____

8.10 → ACTION
I make _____ effort to avoid buying furniture and other items made from tropical wood, unless they clearly state that they are produced by sustainable methods.

1. no	0
2. a little	3
3. a moderate	6
4. a good	9
5. an extensive	12

My Score_____

☞ Tropical rainforests, which are responsible for 70% of the biomass that keeps the earth from warming (the greenhouse effect) and which are the potential source of thousands of medically important products, are being cut at a rate of 4% per year. That is roughly the area of the state of Pennsylvania. Much of this cutting is done to meet the demand for wood products and raising beef in the U.S. and other developed countries (land is cleared for cattle grazing).

Common tropical woods that are endangered include Amazaque, andiroba, apitong, ebony, gaboon, iroko, jelutong, kapur, kempas, lauan/meranti, lignumvitae, macawood, mahogany, Merbau, Nyatoh, Mexican oak, obeche, piquia, ramin, sapele, utile, and wenge.

North American hardwoods that are decorative and durable and can substitute for tropical woods include ash, red birch, cherry, bird's-eye maple, myrtle, red and white oaks, English brown oak, pear, and walnut.

About 20% of the world's oxygen is produced in the Amazon rainforest. However, that estimate will be outdated in the near future at the current rate of deforestation. Rainforests once occupied 15% of the earth's surface and now they occupy 6%. Scientists estimate that if the current rates of deforestation continue - 2.4 acres per second (the equivalent of 2 football fields) and 78 million acres per year (an area larger than the country of Poland) - by the year 2030 basically all of our precious and unique tropical rainforest ecosystems will be destroyed.

****

Total Your Scores For Section 8

❏ IMPACT_____
➔ ACTION_____

Section 9
Toxics

The average U.S. Home generates 15 pounds of hazardous waste each year. The following chart shows the breakdown from the early 1990's by types of waste:

      30% - Oil paints and related products
      18% - Motor oil
      16% - Latex paints
      14% - Cleaners
      11% - Pesticides
      11% - Miscellaneous (adhesives, batteries, maintenance products...)

When hazardous materials are improperly disposed of in landfills, they can leach into waterways seriously damaging ecosystems and endangering human health. This section evaluates your efforts to minimize the use of toxic products and to dispose of them properly.

9.1 ❑ IMPACT

I make _____ effort to keep hazardous wastes (old batteries, solvents, used motor oil, paints, pesticides and so on) from going into the garbage or sewer and to take these items to a hazardous waste collection point.

1. no	32
2. a little	24
3. a moderate	16
4. a good	8
5. an extensive	4

My Score_____

☛The Environmental Protection Agency has designated the following chemicals as toxic enemies 1 through 16. Check labels for these products. Many, however, are "hidden" secondary products in the manufacture of products you buy; five of the sixteen for example, are hidden in the manufacture of plastics.

1. Benzene
2. Cadmium and its compounds
3. Carbon tetrachloride
4. Chloroform
5. Chromium and its compounds
6. Cyanides
7. Dichloromethane
8. Lead and its compounds
9. Nickel and its compounds
10. Methylethyl ketone
11. Tetrachloroethylene
12. Toluene
13. 1, 1, 1-trichloroethane
14. Trichloroethylene
15. Mercury and its compounds
16. Xylene(s)

Nickel/cadmium (NiCad) batteries thrown away by consumers are the single largest source of cadmium pollution (toxic heavy metal) in the environment. Most rechargeable batteries are NiCad, including built-in batteries such as those in camcorders and other rechargeable electronic devices. Never throw away NiCad batteries or devices such as cell phones or laptop computers and PDA's that contain rechargeable batteries. Take them to a hazardous waste collection site for proper disposal.

9.2 ❏ IMPACT

My lawn, garden, or home is ____ sprayed with herbicides or pesticides.

1. never	0
2. rarely	2
3. occasionally (once/yr.)	4
4. regularly (once/mo.)	6
5. frequently (once/wk.)	8

My Score_____

****

9.3 ❏ IMPACT

I am a ___ user of strong household maintenance products such as cleansers and polishes.

1. negligible	1
2. small	3
3. moderate	6
4. frequent	9
5. heavy	12

My Score_____

☞The harmful ingredients here are chlorine, phenols, formaldehyde, cresol, and the benzenes commonly found in household maintenance products. Look for these on the label (they may be hidden in long words like p-dichlorobenzene or pentachlorophenol). Many of these cause cancer and can find their way back into your drinking water if disposed of in the sewer system.

****

9.4 ❏ IMPACT
I am a _____ user of solvent-based compounds such as paints, paint removers, varnishes, cleaning chemicals, and so on.

1. negligible	0
2. small	4
3. moderate	8
4. moderately heavy	16
5. heavy	24

My Score_____

9.5 ❏ IMPACT

I am a _____ user of dry cleaners.

1.	negligible	0
2.	small	1
3.	moderate	2
4.	frequent	3
5.	heavy	4

My Score_____

☛ Dry cleaning generates large amounts of toxic waste from the use of perchlorethylene, or "perc", the main cleaning agent. New methods of dry cleaning are being developed using biodegradable cleaners. Ask your *Green* dry cleaner about the process.

9.6 ❏ IMPACT

I use non-phosphate laundry soap _____.

1. always	1
2. most of the time	2
3. half of the time	3
4. sometimes	4
5. never/rarely	5

My Score_____

☛Phosphate is not a toxic compound, but it is a pollutant because it stimulates algal growth that depletes the oxygen levels of waterways, leading to suffocation of fish. Many brand-name detergents now available in supermarkets have no phosphate in them. Check the ingredient label.

9.7 ❏ IMPACT
I have air-conditioning_____.

1. in neither my car nor my house	0
2. in my car or house, but it's non-CFC	2
3. in my car or house	4
4. in more than one car	6
5. in my car(s) and my house	8

My Score_____

☛Chlorofluorocarbons (CFCs) that are used in air-conditioning systems are a major cause of the loss of the ozone layer. The United States has 5% of the world's population, but contributes 29% of the world's CFCs to the atmosphere.

Most damaging to the ozone layer are the R-12 CFCs. Until recently air conditioning and refrigeration systems contained R-12 CFCs. New systems use non-CFCs. You can arrange to have

CFCs from your car recycled, and replaced with non-CFC compounds. Most urban areas have car air-conditioning repair businesses that can drain and then recycle or destroy the dangerous compounds and replace them with more environmentally friendly ones.

****

9.8 ❑ IMPACT
I make sure that my motor oil gets recycled, that my old car batteries get recycled, and that my drained antifreeze is either recycled or taken to a hazardous waste collection point.

1. all of the above/true	1
2. two of the above/true	2
3. one of the above/true	3
4. none of the above/true	6

My Score_____

☛Used motor oil is considered hazardous waste and has a high disposal cost.
According to the U.S. Environmental

Protection Agency, the largest single source of oil pollution fouling our nation's waters is not tanker spills (including the Exxon Valdez), but used motor oil dumped by home mechanics. Additionally, each day Americans throw away an estimated 90,000 oil filters.

****

9.9 ❑ IMPACT
The sewer system my house is connected with causes _____ problems by leaking or discharging raw sewage into the waterways or groundwater systems. (This question is a concern primarily for people with septic tank sewage systems)

1. no	4
2. little or infrequent	8
3. occasional	16
4. frequent	32
5. frequent & serious	48

My Score_____

9.10 → ACTION
I make _____ effort to use environmentally friendly, low-toxicity cleaning and household maintenance products or methods.

1. no	0
2. a little	4
3. a moderate	8
4. a good	16
5. an extensive	32

My Score_____

****

9.11 → ACTION
I make __ effort to tolerate occasional insects or weeds around my home and to control them using environmentally friendly methods.

1. no	0
2. a little	1
3. a moderate	2
4. a good	4
5. an extensive	8

My Score_____

9.12 → ACTION
I make _____ effort to use non-solvent-based paints and other compounds.

1. no	0
2. a little	2
3. a moderate	4
4. a good	8
5. an extensive	16

My Score_____

****

9.13 → ACTION
When I want to purchase an item such as foam-filled furniture, I make _____ effort to find out if the product has been manufactured without using CFCs.

1. no	0
2. a little	4
3. a moderate	8
4. a good	12
5. an extensive	16

My Score_____

☛Foams that are manufactured without CFCs are Ultracel, Hyperlite, and Geolite. Fire extinguishers that use halons have CFCs. Dry chemical or sodium bicarbonate extinguishers do not use halons and are commonly available.

****

9.14 → ACTION
I buy recycled (re-refined) motor oil for ____ % of my oil needs.

1. 0	0
2. 1-25	1
3. 25-50	2
4. 50-75	3
5. 75-100	4

My Score_____

☛Recycling (re-refining) motor oil has been compared to washing clothes: You don't need to discard clothing the first time it gets dirty. In the same way that clothes are washed, motor oil is cleaned and this re-refined motor oil is available at many of the larger discount auto stores. Synthetic oils, which reduce the need for oil changes by increasing mileage per oil change, also are available.

Total Your Scores For Section 9

❏ IMPACT_____

→ ACTION_____

Section 10
Waste, Packaging, Single-Use Items, and Recycling

Americans produce more than twice as much waste (around 4.5 lbs/day x 0.381 lbs/day of paper) as our nearest "competitors" in waste production -- Germany and Japan (1.7 pounds), and up to 30 times more than individuals in many other countries.

Eighty percent of our waste goes to landfills, more than half of which will be filled up within 10 years. According to 2006 U.S. EPA figures, we recycle only about 32.5% of our waste. This section evaluates your efforts to minimize waste and to recycle.

10.1 ❑ IMPACT

I am a _____ shopper/buyer of packaged or throwaway goods. (Families: Divide total expenditures by the number of adults.)

1. very light ($50 month
   average or less)   5
2. light ($50 to $150
   month average)   10
3. moderate ($150-$300
   month average)   15
4. moderately heavy
   ($300-$500 month average) 20
5. heavy ($500-$800
   month average)   25
6. very heavy
   ($800 plus month average) 30

My Score_____

☛ Packaging accounts for a significant portion of municipal solid waste (MSW) in the form of paper and plastics that take up landfill space.

10.2 ❑ IMPACT

I eat _____ fast-food meals per month.

1. 0-3	2
2. 4-7	4
3. 8-15	6
4. 16-30	8
5. more than 30	10

My Score_____

☛Eating in restaurants that use washable dishware (rather than disposable) is generally even more environmentally efficient than eating at home, because of volume and scale. If you do eat in fast food restaurants, you can ask to be served without cardboard and polystyrene foam containers.

10.3 ❏ IMPACT

I am a _____ consumer of canned or bottled beverages during summer.

1. light (0-2/wk.)	1
2. moderate (3-6/wk.)	2
3. moderately heavy (7-14/wk.)	3
4. heavy (15-21/wk.)	4
5. very heavy (more than 21/wk.)	5

My Score_____

☛ Carry a stainless steel water bottle in your car or in your day bag to avoid having to buy beverages from single-use containers.

10.4 ❏ IMPACT
I recycle _____ % of my aluminum.

1. 80-100	2
2. 60-80	4
3. 40-60	6
4. 20-40	8
5. 0-20	10

My Score_____

☛Recycling aluminum saves 95% of the energy cost of production, and reduces 95% of the air pollution and 97% of the water pollution.
****

10.5 ❏ IMPACT
I recycle_____% of my glass.

1. 80-100	2
2. 60-80	4
3. 40-60	6
4. 20-40	8
5. 0-20	10

My Score_____

☛Recycling glass saves 50% of the raw materials, 50% of the water, and 33% of the energy, and it reduces air pollution by 20%. Using refillable bottles saves four times the energy of using new bottles and 100% on materials. In addition, states with bottle deposit laws have 30-40% less litter.

When depositing used bottles for recycling, keep colors separate or refrain from breaking bottles so that the colors can be separated at the recycling point.

****

10.6 ❏ IMPACT
I recycle _____% of my paper.

1. 80-100		2
2. 60-80		4
3. 40-60		6
4. 20-40		8
5. 0-20		10

My Score_____

☛Major recycling classifications include newspapers, white paper, colored paper, chipboard, and corrugated cardboard. For every 150 pounds of paper you recycle, you save one tree. The average American uses 749 pounds of paper each year.

****

10.7 ❑ IMPACT
I recycle ___% of my recyclable plastic.

1. 80-100	2
2. 60-80	4
3. 40-60	6
4. 20-40	8
5. 0-20	10

My Score_____

☛When faced with a packaging choice, to be environmentally friendly, choose aluminum or glass over plastic.

Following are five reasons to reduce your plastic consumption:

(1) The manufacture of plastic generates 5 of the 6 hazardous wastes the EPA has designated as the worst problem chemicals (propylene, phenol, ethylene, polystyrene, and benzene).

(2) Of the 10 worst polluting companies in the United States, 6 are involved in the manufacture of plastics or plastic-related compounds.

(3) Plastic can last for centuries in landfills.

(4) Most of the plastic you "recycle" does not actually get "recycled". Some of it may find its way into asphalt, product filler, other low-value products or worse, the landfill. Only a small percentage of recycled plastic goes back into making containers.

(5) Chemicals in plastic containers leach into the food and beverages that we consume and have been linked to cancer and other diseases.

10.8 ❏ IMPACT

I compost_____.

1. neither kitchen nor yard wastes	12
2. kitchen or yard wastes, but not both	6
3. both kitchen and yard wastes	0

My Score_____

☛Find out if your city has a composting program for yard waste or if it takes them to landfills. If your city composts yard waste, then answer either 2 or 3 above.

Composting food and other kitchen waste can decrease the weight of your garbage by 30%-50%. Yard waste is the second biggest component of landfills, after paper. In the fall, 75% of the garbage taken to landfills is made up of leaves. After being taken to landfills, these organic materials can never be recycled back to the land because they become mixed with toxic garbage.

10.9 ❑ IMPACT

I recycle _____ % of my corrugated cardboard.

1. 80-100	2
2. 60-80	4
3. 40-60	6
4. 20-40	8
5. 0-20	10

My Score_____

☛ Ask your waste-removal company if it recycles the cardboard you throw out. Large stores often have bins for cardboard outside the back of the store, and this cardboard is recycled.

10.10 → ACTION
I make _____ effort to avoid buying over-packaged products and to let companies know that I will not buy their products if they over packaged.

1. no	0
2. a little	3
3. a moderate	6
4. a good	9
5. an extensive	12

My Score_____

☛The solid waste flow for the average person in this country is as follows according to 2006 data from EPA: Total Waste Generated:

33.9%	paper & paperboard
12.9%	yard waste
12.4%	food waste
11.7%	plastics
7.6%	metals
5.3%	glass
7.3%	textiles, rubber, leather
5.5%	wood
3.3%	other

Since 1960, our per capita generation of municipal solid waste has increased from 2.68/day to 4.6/day in 2006; even though our recycling rates have increased to more than 28% nationwide.

Try your best to practice the four R's of waste reduction: Refuse, Reduce, Reuse, (refurbish and repair) and when all else fails, Recycle.

****

10.11 → ACTION

When alternatives are available, I make ___ effort to avoid eating food or drinking beverages served in single-serving, throw-away containers.

1. no	0
2. a little	2
3. a moderate	4
4. a good	6
5. an extensive	8

My Score_____

☛Have you thought about the fact that a plastic spoon or fork has an average-use life of about 3 minutes and geological life in the landfill of a century or more?

****

10.12 → ACTION
I carry utensils to use rather than employing single-use items.

1. never	0
2. mug, sometimes	2
3. mug, most of the time	4
4. mug, spoon, fork- sometimes	6
5. mug, spoon, fork- most of the time	8

My Score_____

☛Light and durable utensils that are easy to take with you to the restaurant.

10.13 → ACTION

I ____take my own cloth or used grocery bags to the grocery store for bagging items.

1. never	0
2. rarely	1
3. sometimes	2
4. frequently	3
5. always	4

My Score_____

☛Do not underestimate the effect you can have on other people when they see you taking this kind of action.

10.14 → ACTION

When I have any construction done, or when I do a major house cleanup, or when I move, I make____ effort to minimize the amount of waste going into dumpsters.

1. no	0
2. a little	2
3. a moderate	4
4. a good	6
5. an extensive	8

My Score_____

☛Home projects such as major cleanups and renovations can generate huge amounts of waste. See how much of it you can repurpose, find a new home for or donate. Dealing with environmental concerns at times like these can be difficult because they are often times of stress and hurry. So plan ahead.

10.15 → ACTION

I buy retreaded tires for ___ % of my automotive tire needs.

1. 0	0
2. up to 25%	2
3. 25% to 50%	4
4. 50% to 75%	6
5. 75% to 100%	8

My Score_____

☞Tire disposal is a big problem, with more than 250 million scrap tires generated a year in the US. By purchasing retreaded tires, you keep tires out of these dumps. According to John Serumgard, chair of the Scrap Tire Management Council, retreaded tires are every bit as safe as new tires.

Total Your Scores For Section 10

❏ IMPACT_____

→ ACTION_____

Section 11
Environmental Advocacy

There are three significant ways to change environmental management policies in corporations: (1) through selective buying, (2) by advocating government regulation, and (3) through direct actions such as making telephone calls, writing letters or fostering public awareness. This section counts what you do in (2) and (3). Do not underestimate the effectiveness of writing letters and doing public advocacy work for the environment.

11.1 → ACTION
I make _____ effort be informed about state and local legislative activities relevant to the environment and to make phone calls to my legislators at critical times.

1. no	0
2. a little	4
3. a moderate	8
4. a good	12
5. an extensive	16

My Score_____

****

11.2 → ACTION
I write approximately _____ letter(s) per year to my government representatives regarding environmental issues.

1. 0	0
2. 1	10
3. 2-3	12
4. 4-6	14
5. more than 6	16

My Score_____

☛Writing just one letter per year makes a big difference. Note how this is reflected in the points.

****

11.3 → ACTION
I vote ___ % of the time. (This counts all elections: federal, state, local, and, if you are a student, school.)

1. 0-20%	0
2. 20%-40%	4
3. 40%-60%	8
4. 60%-80%	12
5. 80%-100%	16

My Score_____

****

11.4 → ACTION
I volunteer _____ hours per year to support environmental activities such as cleanups, tree planting, water monitoring, community organizing, committees, fund-raising, and so on.

1. 0	4
3. 10-25	8
4. 25-50	12
5. 50-100	16
6. 100-200	24
7. 200-400	32

My Score_____

****

11.5 → ACTION
I donate $_____ per year to environmental groups or concerns. (Include money spent on membership dues and subscriptions for environmental organizations.)

1. 0-10	0
2. 10-25	3
3. 25-50	6
4. 50-100	9
5. 100-200	12
6. more than 200	16

My Score_____

11.6 → ACTION

I make ____ effort to communicate my environmental concerns to key people such as local city council persons, store managers, administrators, business owners, and so on.

1. no	0
2. a little	4
3. a moderate	8
4. a good	12
5. an extensive	16

My Score_____

****

11.7 → ACTION

Of my financial investments ____ % are in "green" portfolios.

1. 0 (or no investments)	0
2. 1-20	2
20-40	4
)-60	8
80	12
)0	16

My Score_____

☛ In a rapidly growing field of "green investing", dozens of funds exist that invest only in corporations with good environmental records.

If you do not invest, you can still have an impact on investments. Virtually all city, county, and state governments have investments, as does your pension fund.

Total Your Scores For Section 11

→ ACTION_____

Section 12
Land Stewardship

This section counts your direct impact on the land. Although our indirect impacts are generally of higher magnitude, we also directly affect the land and its ecosystems in many ways.

Try to visualize how you affect the ecosystem in which you live. When you do this, small actions that seem insignificant, like getting rid of some "unsightly" shrubs in a corner of your backyard, may actually turn out to be harmful to an ecosystem. Do the shrubs provide habitat for birds? Do they provide an overwintering site for certain beneficial insects that eat garden pests during the summer? These questions may take years for you to answer, but being aware of them is a first step.

12.1 ❑ IMPACT

The soil erosion on my property is _____.

1. insignificant/N.A.	0
2. very small	1
3. small	2
4. moderate	3
5. often fairly serious	6
6. often very serious	12

My Score_____

****

12.2 ❑ IMPACT

I do _____ miles of off-road driving or motorcycling per year on land that has no existing track.

1. 0	0
2. 1-25	2
3. 25-100	4
4. 100-500	6
5. more than 500	8

My Score_____

12.3 → ACTION
When I hike in natural areas, I make ____ effort to stay on existing trails and to make a minimum impact, especially on land that is wet or fragile.

1. no	0
2. a little	2
3. a moderate	4
4. a good	6
5. an extensive	8

My Score_____

12.4 → ACTION

I make _____ effort to leave part of my land (whether backyard or extensive property), to grow wild for wildlife habitat.

1. no	0
2. a little	2
3. a moderate	4
4. a good	6
5. an extensive	8

My Score_____

Total Your Scores For Section 12

❏ IMPACT_____

→ ACTION_____

Section 13
Livelihood

For those who are able, one of the most important ways to make a difference to the earth is to leave organizations that are environmentally destructive. Many companies are making fundamental changes in their operations to minimize their environmental impact. Making changes within your work environment can be just as effective as changing careers. One suggestion to a supervisor could bring about an environmental impact reduction that would dwarf all the changes you make in your personal life.

****

13.1 → ACTION
I have made or am making _____ effort to develop a livelihood that is earth-friendly or is with an earth-friendly company or organization.

1. no/very little	0
2. a little	8
3. a moderate	16
4. a good	32
5. an extensive	48

My Score_____

****

13.2 → ACTION
I have made or am making _____ effort to bring about changes that reduce the environmental impact of my company, department, or office.

1. no/very little	0
2. a little	4
3. a moderate	8
4. a good	12
5. an extensive	16

My Score_____

****

Total Your Scores For Section 13

→ ACTION_____

Section 14
Family Planning

There are only two questions in this last section, but they are enormously important ones; note the magnitude of the points. The number of children you have creates your biggest environmental impact. This is not to say that having children is bad, one or two children brought up by anyone who cares enough to use this book is most probably a positive contribution to the world. We need educated and aware people to lead the world and make their mark on the next generation.

14.1 ❑ IMPACT

I plan to have _____ children. (If you already have children, ask them to answer this question.)

1. 0	0
2. 1	10
3. 2	50
4. 3	500
5. 4 or more	5,000

My Score_____

☛ Population growth is exponential, which means that large numbers are reached after just a few generations.

Limiting population growth is especially important in the United States. 2002 statistics from World Population Balance indicate one American uses as much energy as: 2 Japanese, 6 Mexicans, 13 Chinese, 31 Indians, 128 Bangladeshis, 307 Tanzanians, or 307 Ethiopians. This illustrates why it is important that we, in the United States, focus on our own population problem before worrying about other countries.

14.2 → ACTION
I plan to or am making ___ effort to raise my children in an environmentally sensible way and to set a good example for them.

1. very little	0
2. some	6
3. a moderate (sporadic)	12
4. a moderate (sustained)	24
5. an extensive (sustained)	48

My Score_____

Total Your Scores For Section 14

❑ IMPACT_____

→ ACTION_____

How Green Am I?

How Green Am I? Totals

Total the points for all sections:

	IMPACT	ACTION
1. Household Energy: General	_____	_____
2. Household Energy: Winter	_____	_____
3. Household Energy: Summer	_____	_____
4. Water	_____	_____
5. Transportation Consumerism:	_____	_____
6. Durable Goods Consumerism:	_____	_____
7. Food & Agricultural Products	_____	_____

8. Consumerism: Paper
   & Forest Products   _____   _____

9. Toxics   _____   _____

10. Waste, Packaging,
    Single-Use Items,
    and Recycling   _____   _____

11. Environmental
    Advocacy   _____   _____

12. Land Stewardship   _____   _____

13. Livelihood   _____   _____

14. Family Planning   _____   _____

Your Score
Totals   _____   _____

Now you can see what kind of an eco-logical footprint you are making among the following 8 categories and where you sit on the "Action" continuum:

Impact Rating	Points
Eco-Titan	150 or less
Eco-Hero	151-225
Eco-Mentor	226-275
Eco-Average Citizen	276-350
Eco-Slowpoke	351-450
Eco-Frankenstein	451-600
Eco-Sherman Tank	601-750
Eco-Tyrannosaurus Rex (bound for extinction)	over 750

Action Rating	Points
I could do better!	0-100
Good	101-200
Very Good	201-300
Excellent	301-400
Earth Action Hero	400 plus

Congratulations on finishing
How Green Am I?! "So now what?"

Begin by choosing the area that holds the most interest for you because passion most often equates to action. Set reasonable goals to avoid getting overwhelmed and giving up. Many small steps add up to a long and successful journey. And be sure to share with others along the way. It will keep you engaged and encourage those closest to you to start their own journey toward a greener lifestyle. Remember my Cardinal Rule, "Living a green lifestyle is not about suffering or doing without." If we are to create a green lifestyle that works for us it cannot be based on suffering in any way. So remember to have fun with this. Enjoy stretching your ability to live green.

To help you measure your progress, be sure to save your scores and complete the *How Green Am I?* process again in 6 months to 1 year, then annually after that. You can use a different colored pencil each time you review then enjoy seeing the progress you are making along the way.